my first fruits
in ancient greek

translated by Joshua Duvall

polyglot kids

μῆλον

mēlon

apple

ἄπιον

ápion

pear

σταφυλή

staphulé

grape

σῦκον

súkon

fig

συκάμινον

sūkámīnon

mulberry

προῦνον

proúnon

plum

κερασός

kerasós

cherry

μῆλον περσικόν

mélon persikón

peach

ῥόα

rhóa

pomegranate

μηλοπέπων

mēlopépōn

melon

© 2025 by Polyglot Kids Books / World Poetry Books
Photography © 2025 by Sebastian Fröhlich

Series editors: Peter Constantine & Hannes Schumacher
Translated into Ancient Greek by Joshua Duvall
Photography: Sebastian Fröhlich
Design: Hannes Schumacher & Sebastian Fröhlich
ISBN: 978-1-967821-00-6

Polyglot Kids Books is an imprint of World Poetry Books, Inc. New York.

This publication was made possible with the support of Carlucci's Fund.

www.ingramcontent.com/pod-product-compliance
Lightning Source LLC
Chambersburg PA
CBHW062022050526
44107CB00106B/941